JOHN HYDE
a Faustian comedy

a verse play by

Ronald Garbin

Finishing Line Press
Georgetown, Kentucky

JOHN HYDE
a Faustian comedy

Publisher: Leah Maines

Editor: Christen Kincaid

Cover Art: Mary Garbin

Author Photo: Mary Garbin

Printed in the USA on acid-free paper.
Order online: www.finishinglinepress.com
                also available on amazon.com

Author inquiries and mail orders:
Finishing Line Press
P. O. Box 1626
Georgetown, Kentucky 40324
U. S. A.

Synopsis of *John Hyde*

To corrupt his depressed country's currency, anti-hero President John Hyde schemes with Dr. La Brea, his satanic backer, to foster a Faustian program of spending 3-dollar bills called "The Modern Deal." Hyde kills an opposed Court Justice, and to fill his vacancy names a former friend Frances Harkins, a judge in a local case against Helen Scopes, Hyde's promised amour. Helen is charged for teaching school children his doctrine of "monkey spending" in violation of a local ordinance. The plot starts going wrong—or right. Frances, Helen, and Mrs. Hyde welcome news of economic recovery, and credit Hyde. Before midnight tolls La Brea's deadline, Hyde tries planting counterfeit and arson to reverse the reversal.

Cast of Characters for JOHN HYDE

John Hyde... President

Dr. La Brea .... Hyde's physician and political backer

Helen Scopes née Troy .... a nature lobbyist

Frances Harkins... Supreme Court nominee

Lucy.. Hyde's wife

Leonard Bosky .... a Treasury Agent

Daisy Lyons ....a nurse and part-time artist

Waldo Waldo... a would-be assassin

Stonewall Crabbe.................... a reactionary Supreme Court Justice

NOTE: The number 9 of actors reduces to just 7 if one person
plays both Helen and Daisy, while another plays both Crabbe

Time and place

A capital city during a depression.

Three settings

SCENE 1: the home of Justice Crabbe.

SCENE 2: the White House, weeks later.

SCENE 3: an insane asylum, days later.

SCENE 4: the White House, hours later.

Character Sketches for *John Hyde*

Stonewall Crabbe—As Court Chief Justice, he totally opposes Hyde's Modern Deal and its spendthrift notions. Facing Hyde in person might well provoke the Judge's heart failure.

Initially Crabbe's nurse, **Daisy Lyons**—has empathy for patients, but also a part-time artistic interest in their final hours.

The Republic's President **John Reynard Hyde**—fully defines himself as a villain with no sure existence beyond his Faustian bargain with Dr. La Brea, which requires Hyde as President to destroy the nation's currency. The mission has completely absorbed his character, as an actor into his role.

Lucy Hyde—First lady, she feels continually baffled by her husband, and perhaps remains so on her turning point journey for a divorce.

Former Labor Secretary **Frances Harkins**—now serves only as judge in a local courthouse where Helen Scopes comes to trial for teaching Hyde's program of spending without saving. This test case contributes to the conflict.

Lamont La Brea—figures as Hyde's evil angel and backer, though he lacks his trained client's detailed technical know-how in economics. Also he has no idea of the providence of Helen, his supposed minion.

Helen Scopes nee Troy—a beauteous young widow supposedly promised Hyde as part of his Faustian bargain with La Brea, but she emerges with a far different function.

Treasury Agent **Leonard Bosky**—has competence and responsibility to a point, but remains as clueless about the unfolding of Hyde's agenda, as Hyde does himself until the last.

Insane would-be assassin **Waldo Waldo**—seems safely incarcerated after his first attempt at murder, but has cunning to dramatize his own cure and escape for another attempt.

SCENE 1

A room in the house of JUSTICE STONEWALL CRABBE. The JUSTICE enters sitting in a wheel chair pushed by DAISY now dressed in a nurse's uniform.

DAISY
Shall I fluff up your pillow, Justice Crabbe?

CRABBE
No, it's already soft as spineless mush!
Nowadays the Court had better show backbone
against newfangled economic fads.
As long as I sit on the highest Bench
I won't use pillows to hold up my head.

DAISY
And yet you mustn't aggravate yourself
with sudden dire exerting of your heart.
Remember doctor's orders: take it easy.

CRABBE
Just leave the pillow, hussy! Never mind
either my head or heart, let both of them
be hard as slate, the more that modern vice
waxes and bubbles, the more old-fashioned virtue
should stand as marble. All the doctors warn
don't get too hot or cold, tired, sick or old.
Much good their orders are! I woke and saw
this morning staring at me in my bed
a woman with apocalyptic eyes
so fearsome that I stirred and called aloud!

DAISY
Heavens! you must have wakened from a nightmare.

CRABBE
I never saw her like on land or sea.
Her hair was gold, her skin blanched chalky white;
She stared and smiled at me so deathly grim
it chilled my bones, and stood my hair on end.

CRABBE (Continued)
She offered me some medicine to drink,
saying a polluted river made me sick.

DAISY
Polluted river doesn't make much sense.

CRABBE
It does with all the greenbacks washing over
society like scraps of rotten cod
against a tainted shore. The woman warned me
to dam the flood of spurious currency,
or bear the consequences to my grave.
Of course our jester president has loosed
a stream of tainted money on the land
with no redemption value based on gold.
For now the so-called President, John Hyde,
proposes to debase our legal tender
by printing greenback paper he will scatter
like falling leaves his gall calls charity,
though not a single ingot has he got
to back such money. He will wreck the state!

DAISY
Hush! Calm yourself, please.

CRABBE
                          I tell you, Nurse Daisy,
this president warps not our money only,
but moral life. His doctrine is a scam
upon the populace. Three-dollar bills!
Three-dollar bills he issues gray and green
as currency without a solid base of
precious metal. He corrupts us all!

(*CRABBE wheels himself about.*)

DAISY
Shush! Easy, easy.

DAISY (Continued)
The country, after all, was in depression.

CRABBE
Was?—Is! Because the pace of manufactures
had ebbed so low our White House Hyde proposed
that burning surplus goods would bolster prices.
The unemployed marched on the Capitol
halting the conflagration, though the man
himself dismissed the multitude's unrest,
pooh-poohed the market crash that panic caused
because a radio drama had broadcast
tales of invading Martians reaching earth
had landed on Wall Street and crashed the Market.
He told them the economy is sound,
and not to think the Martian rumors real,
which calmed them down, but worse could follow yet.

DAISY
You mustn't fret about this any more.
You'll make your illness worse.

CRABBE
                              It beats in my mind.
Four full years Hyde marked time. To end depression
demanded scrimping. Hyde just temporized.
Though he declared for balancing the budget,
which economic axioms require,
the budget keeps inflating with red ink.
The country needs a sound and solid dollar,
and full recovery demands that we enforce
a strict austerity, but now that Hyde
escaped assassination his prestige
amounts to that of almost any martyr.

DAISY
Because that Waldo person shot at him,
although a demonstrator spoiled his aim.

CRABBE
Yes, Mr. Bosky, interrupted death,
which left Hyde grateful.

DAISY
He revised his program.

CRABBE
Yes!
And promised more largesse. So now begins
his great corruption called the Modern Deal:
corrupting money, morals, citizens.
For Hyde shirks thrift, and spends beyond the budget,
till public doles and handouts must become
habitual panaceas, mother's milk.

DAISY
But surely people are too poor to pay
for goods at higher prices. It makes no sense,
with gutters glutted full of derelicts,
millions of people unemployed and hungry,
while from the chins of the rich come dribbling down
nothing but promises that higher prices
might do us any good. Sir, I was there.
A sardine could sooner walk to Palestine
than we could walk that road of burning goods
to any good result. Jobs have gone missing:
dishwashers, waitresses, clerks, salesmen, teachers,
are out of work in every walk of life;
laid off, foreclosed, broke, on a holiday.
At my bank I stood hours in line to draw
my savings out of my account, and then
the teller shut the window in my face!
All the gold eagles of my nest egg fled
like dodos somewhere else. The bank went bust.
To borrow any money now demands
an actual Martian with some cash to spare.
I try to put the bite on people now,
and they bite back! Few folks have savings left.

DAISY (Continued)
Of course we picketed for some relief.

CRABBE
So you were in that host of unemployed.
Young woman, it did you no credit marching
against those marshals seeking for those goods
a real resuscitation of their price.
Hyde's halting the incineration will
frame a future to our lasting cost,
set termites gnawing at the Capitol,
and make you radicals respectable.

DAISY
I'm not a radical, nor were the others.
We voted Mr. Hyde for President
to bring us better times against the pinch.

CRABBE
To march here they abandoned home and hearth,
denying the economy the time
to find an equilibrium again.
Plenty lies at our doorstep, once we solve
the difficulty of its distribution.

DAISY
But isn't that, your Honor, always true?
And I was desperate.

CRABBE
                    You could have come to me.
To have a nurse I could have hired you then.

DAISY
Through your door I couldn't have put a foot
without credentials. A real nurse I'm not.

CRABBE
Not real! Your references claimed otherwise!

DAISY

Well, naturally, I have some background nursing,
but as a stopgap, not my real ambition.
We mustn't argue and make you overtired, then
have to call the doctor.

CRABBE

            Damn the Doctor!
Forget the Doctor. If you're not a nurse
with a professional preference, heart and soul,
what are you then, Miss Lyons? Speak the truth.

DAISY

Me and my big mouth!

CRABBE

            I insist you tell.

DAISY

I want to be an artist, Justice Crabbe;
a painter who primarily does portraits,
portraits of people lingering in illness.

CRABBE

Demons and thunderation!
Painting is how you'd earn a livelihood?

DAISY

I have a flair for portraiture of men,
including public figures—it sounds awful,
but yet it's therapeutic in a way,
and it provides the critics what they want;
and so I'd moonlight at the hospital
the late night shift, which paid for paint and brushes,
and rent of course, and got me introduced
into the *avant-garde* for which I've paid
in lost promotions. The Chief Nurse loathed my sketching;
so when they cut the staff, she let me go.

CRABBE
No doubt as an economizing measure.

DAISY
It doesn't matter, since they also sacked
a lot of patients.

CRABBE
          All this stuns me, nurse.
What should I call you? If these be thy gods,
O Israel, then nothing can sustain us! I don't
know whether to cashier you now
for your artistic pranks, or raise your wages,
or quaver that you make of me your model.
No! Justice Stonewall Crabbe has got to stand
a member of the nation's highest Court,
and I'll be damned to shake at any words
of revelation poured into my ears,
though slick as spit on monuments fresh rain
will wash away. Nurse, you deserve a raise.

DAISY
I can't accept a raise in pay, your Honor.
I haven't told the worst.

CRABBE
          Then out with it,
and no more fluffing: if you wanted me
your subject posed in coffin or on pillow,
I'd do it gladly, once my work is done
of turning back Hyde's program from the Bench.
To send the villain packing means I've lived
through time enough; then paint me to the grave.

DAISY
Oh, don't say that! The President has made
the only effort people think may turn
the tide of breadlines. You have no idea
of what the world outside must call the worst.

DAISY (Continued)
With unrelenting rigor you dismiss
the worst as nothing. Oh, you're so impervious,
I could just shake you! What you call the worst
drove people marching miles for some relief
from unemployment, or what's really worse:
foreclosure, fear, eviction. I was there.
In every face I witnessed angry eyes
glowing as dry as August in a dust storm.
To Mr. Hyde petitioners appealed
for help surviving all you think so light.
The worst made us accept the jobs he offered
paying less gold than paper, which I took.
Oh, yes, I think the worst must lie outside
of your imagining. The worst it was
gave me my first commission: officials took
my sketches to the Treasury engravers for use
in printing the three-dollar bill.

CRABBE
Hyde's folding money!

DAISY
                              Now you know the worst.

CRABBE
So! You designed Hyde's gilded bills of Mammon.
The time has come for your departure, nurse.
Confounded woman, did you come to spy
upon me here for Hyde in my own house?
Downsize yourself! By your deceit you've shown
supreme contempt for law and Constitution.
You'll quit my service. Leave my house.—Get out.

(CRABBE points to a door.)

Back to your master, go. Get out at once!

DAISY
I meant no disrespect, sir, for the Court—

CRABBE
Get out, I say!

(DAISY leaves. CRABBE wheels himself about.)

This is a blow I hardly can sustain.
Hyde usurps history with his Modern Deal:
the Constitution, law, dreams, everything!
Like Gadarene swine, down a steep place rush
the people stumbling, headlong to embrace
the flimsy paper fiat being printed,
and only the Supreme Court can turn back
their mad stampede down to insolvency.
The madman must be stopped. He must be stopped!
No, calmly, calmly. Nurse is right for once:
I've got to take it easy, must relax;
I've got to stay alive on doctor's orders

(HYDE enters the room.)

to force responsibility on Hyde.

HYDE
Good morning, Justice Crabbe. Are you alone?

(CRABBE half stands.)

CRABBE
You!!

HYDE
Yes, Reynard Hyde, your very humble servant.

CRABBE
Pernicious scheming fox, away with you!
Get out of here this minute! Get out! Go,

CRABBE (Continued)
before I call the law! Nurse Lyons! Daisy!

(CRABBE collapses backward into his wheel chair.)

HYDE
She seems to have departed, or perhaps
you just discharged her when you found me out
to be her patron. Both of us she seems
to have deserted, but it makes no matter:
at least she won't disturb us as we seek
an understanding, Stonewall, you and I,
regarding economic policy
to aid the indigent. My program needs
legal endorsement by the Supreme Court.
On that you hold now the deciding vote.

(CRABBE struggles again to his feet.)

CRABBE
You dare ask my support for your mad schemes??
This is an outrage! So we have at last
a whippersnapper president who dreams
of overspending as a royal road
to public riches, and a legal tender
that bears a leering picture of himself,
but has behind it not an ounce of bullion
to bolster what he spends on public works!
Your program spurs a madness that will saddle
descendants with a debt for generations!
You'd leave unpaid for monuments, schools, parks,
museums, galleries, hospitals and highways.
In your vainglorious optimism, sir,
you'd pack the Court, and pulverize the law,
maneuver and contrive to no avail.
Morals and thrift are paramount with me.
I'd sooner abdicate my faculties
than sanction your demented, unbacked bills!

HYDE

My modern scrip is backed by mathematics.
Should every individual household strive
today in private to secure itself
prosperity within its own oasis,
amid a dearth for everybody else,
they would commit a fundamental blunder.
When misers hoard, and prudent people stint
themselves of luxuries, stuffing mattresses
with a few savings, nothing will avail:
each lives a little chip in a great gap
that spreads a desert everywhere about them.
My Secretary of the Treasury,
Henry Gainsborough, first urged that we pinch pennies,
but private thrift would twist the public throat
with tightened tourniquets that choke trade off.
We only thrive by trade with one another
by servicing and goods employing men,
and only so I'll fund the public weal,
build roads and dams, dig irrigation channels,
erect a pyramid, dismantle slums,
and subsidize a new long-distance aircraft.

CRABBE

Waste! Waste and poison! All based on a theory
nobody understands, which hauls on risk.
Confound it, man, it's choking, drowning us!
This folly has to stop!

HYDE

            I've just begun
to stimulate new mines and factories,
and more will follow. I'll print up more bank notes,
and bury them in bottles underground,
hiring workmen to dig them up again,
if I can find no better work for them;
or launch a spacecraft that could strike the moon
with a resounding gong, cash registered.

CRABBE

Sir: not while I live. Over my dead body.

HYDE

Be careful not to strain your heart, old man.

CRABBE

My heart's not strained! Only I stand aghast
that Secretary Harkins' resignation
didn't split your Cabinet wide as the Red Sea.
Let someone bring a suit against your program!
I hope the case reaches the highest Court.

HYDE

Mind what you prate now.

CRABBE

Do you threaten me?

(HYDE leaps on CRABBE and bears him down in the wheel chair
with a pillow over his face.)

Help! Down with paper money, down with it!
Down paper now. Now! . . . Oh, oh!

HYDE

Quiet, quiet, your Honor. Don't exert yourself.
No breath. Limp, limp.

(CRABBE dies. DAISY enters.)

DAISY

What are you doing??

(HYDE climbs off CRABBE.)

HYDE

Done.

I've tried to rouse him, but his pulse is gone.
Our Justice Crabbe has had a heart attack.

(HYDE takes CRABBE's wrist.)

The sad inevitable has occurred.
We must accept it.

> DAISY
>> Justice Crabbe is dead!

> HYDE

He was a man, not the Great Wall of China
that he envisioned. Stonewall tried to keep
out the barbarians from his paradise,
but suffocated from paralysis,
and died of rigor mortis of the mind;
in a paroxysm of outrage, he drew
death to his bedside like a greedy heir.
And now his fat is in the fire, Ms. Lyons;
splinter your wits on that fact!

> DAISY
>> Oh, my God!

My practicing both medicine and art
as my vocation now has really made
a still life of my subject. This is horrid!
We quarreled over politics today,
over my sketching of your portrait, sir,
for which he ordered me to leave the house.
So I touched up his portrait in my room.
Once his eruption ended, I expected
to be called back and waited. Is he dead?

> HYDE

Of rectitude that often heralds death
of the unbending righteous. Never mind.
You must not blame yourself, my dear, for this:
your words upset him less than words of mine.
Even from down the hall, you must have heard
over our politics the arguing.

DAISY

I never should have left him here alone
to brood in anger. I should have soothed his rage.
This time I tried to justify myself,
and so my patient dies of a heart attack!
Oh, this is dreadful! The poor, awful old man!

(As SHE starts to fail, HYDE takes her by the shoulders.)

HYDE

Now, Daisy, no tears, or no longer will
your face deserve a mirror any more
than does my own. Come on now: let me help
find you a glass of water, not your eyes.
Soon they'll be giving better than they get.

DAISY

I do feel faint . . .

(HYDE leads her out.)

END OF SCENE 1

SCENE 2

A room in the White House, not an office. A table set with a tea service. LUCY and FRANCES come in together and sit down.

LUCY
Thank you for coming, Frances, from so far.

FRANCES
I wonder that you found me at a distance.

LUCY
I had to, and I had my various spies.
Let me pour you some tea while I explain.

(LUCY pours tea.)

Since you resigned, I haven't found a soul
I could confide in, other than my spies.
Tell me one thing: why did you leave the Cabinet?

FRANCES
Officially on grounds of health I left.

LUCY
Perhaps your health's improved since John began
his recent program of recovery.
He always credits the advice you gave
for the inception of the Modern Deal,
which he at first opposed. You favored spending,
while he blew hot and cold, and only gave
with his left hand what his right took away.
Now John has altered, thanks in part to you.

FRANCES
To me? No, the attempt upon his life
by a would-be assassin must count more.

LUCY
Of course that surely made a difference also.

FRANCES
When the attempt was foiled, he changed direction.

LUCY
Thank heaven! Then he heeded your advice.

FRANCES
I thought the death attempt perhaps was staged.

LUCY
Staged!

FRANCES
Yes.

LUCY
Oh, Frances, what are you imagining?

FRANCES
The President and I have played at poker,
and my opinion of his deficits
means rather more than any man-in-the-moon's.
Not *my* health, but his own, made me resign.
I mean that when the President resolved
on surplus burning, madam, he dismissed
as cavils everything I urged against it.
I threatened to resign, and then he suffered
what seemed a heart attack. Away I raced
to fetch the Doctor or a glass of water.
But then it dawned on me that he was playing
another of his jokes—the final straw.
Even with reëlection facing him,
he isn't serious. Therefore I resigned.

LUCY
Frances, he wants you to rejoin the Cabinet
as Labor Secretary once again.
Together you and he could save the country.

FRANCES

Madam First Lady, you astonish me.
To my own ears has never come a rumor
of reappointment. Never have I heard
even a hint of wind from his direction.

LUCY

Well, he's distracted—yes, preoccupied
with Helen Scopes that aviation widow
with whom he's at the airfield now to welcome
home from its maiden transatlantic flight
the transport plane designed by her late husband.
And there will be a ticker tape parade
to follow afterward the ceremony
when John congratulates her as the wife
behind her husband's aircraft. John intends
launching a thousand more in coming years.
Can you believe he meant at first to print
her picture on the new three-dollar bill?
but Henry Gainsborough put a stop to that!
Perhaps I shouldn't complain: the solo flight
of a new aircraft perfectly distracts
from the soup kitchens and depression lines.
So John from tub to shower can only sing
his arias in the woman's praises—Lord!
The world's first woman to divorce her spouse.

FRANCES

The first whose spouse's plane traversed the ocean.

LUCY

Well, it was something epic. More tea, Frances?

FRANCES

If we may stop discussing Mrs. Scopes.
I sympathize with what you tell me, madam,
but you look ill. You ought to see a doctor.

LUCY

Too much of doctors I see lately, thank you.
Dr. La Brea, latest we have here
appeared the day that John was nearly killed.
The President was wonderful. He joked
about the campaign, took to heart attempts
to murder him as a constructive form
of criticism; mocked it was my way
of getting rid of him without divorce!
Oh, he apologized, blamed wounded nerves,
told the new Doctor he had borne a shock,
so therefore *I* would need a sedative!
Whenever since John gets upset, he has
Dr. La Brea give a shot of drugs to me.
I'm his pin cushion now, or voodoo doll.

FRANCES

Good heavens, this is horrid! I'd no idea.

LUCY

Out in the country, in your rural courthouse,
of course you might not hear of such a thing.
The President's favor somehow I have lost.
But now I have a plan that may restore
me to his graces, and you to the Cabinet.
The country needs your services again;
John also wants them, Frances; and I dream
of my surprising him by your return.
He doesn't know that I invited you.

FRANCES

The invitation isn't even his!
good heavens, he doesn't know! Can you be serious?

LUCY

This invitation is my own idea.

FRANCES

Divorce him, Lucy. Sue him for divorce.

FRANCES (Continued)
If you're so desperate, you must straightaway
divorce the man.

LUCY
              But that's unthinkable!
To the electorate for the First Lady
to have a household other than her husband's
would constitute a scandal in the land.
To even urge my leaving derogates
the Chief Executive who steers the state.
Besides, I couldn't possibly run off.
You don't know what it is to be his slave.

FRANCES
Oh, yes, I do, did, packed my bags and left
my resignation drying on his desk.
And you can do the like thing, Lucy: go.

LUCY
If only I could dare! But I could never
 just steal away, but only dream of it.
My life has taken such a silly turn.

FRANCES
It's only silly clinging to the thought
a President elected to his job
as holding an hereditary right
of veto power over common sense.
These Chief Executives are only men,
one like another, though the media bleat
about their differences, it's mostly tripe,
for there are plenty more where they come from,
and in the sea are fish as good as any
extracted in the past. Be selfish then.
Quit living merely as your husband's fool:
Lucy, his goose, on whom not sun nor shade
may throw relief, since you have no real life,
and that's just nothing. You should leave the man.

(HYDE comes in with HELEN and LA BREA.)

LUCY
It's unimaginable. Stop it, Frances!
You've said enough.

HYDE
   Said what, dear?

LUCY
        Hello, Reynard.
Only some hints about a recipe
that Frances recommends for us to try.

HYDE
Frances! My dear Judge Harkins—Please forgive
my negligence. I only just returned
from the airfield, and I had no idea
that you were visiting. This is Helen Scopes.
Her late great husband's cargo plane has flown
nonstop the ocean. Just imagine, Lucy,
what an extraordinary feat that is!

LUCY
So good of you to visit, Mrs. Scopes.
I know you miss your husband.

(THEY shake hands.)

HELEN
        Madam, yes,
but at least christening his cargo plane
the Hectorcraft enshrines his memory.

HYDE
And this is Frances Harkins, an old friend.

HELEN
Judge Harkins and I have already met.

HELEN (Continued)
Your Honor.

FRANCES
Mrs. Scopes.

HYDE
                    Already met!
Well, I had no idea—Did you, Doctor?
Dr. La Brea, this is Frances Harkins.

(FRANCES and LA BREA shake hands.)

LA BREA
How do you do, my dear Judge Harkins—or
should one address you now as Justice Harkins?
Delighted either way that now I meet
the woman nominated to succeed
old Justice Crabbe on this new Supreme Court.

FRANCES
On the Supreme Court! Is this another joke?

HYDE
No, Frances: at the airfield I announced
your nomination maybe on an impulse,
but hardly as a joke. We welcomed home
an epic aircraft, subsidized by us,
as once you recommended. There we waited,
I with some flowers, and Helen with champagne
to smash across the cowling of the plane.
It touched the tarmac, skidding to a stop.
Right then it flashed on me to nominate
you to the Highest Court. Congratulations!

FRANCES
I can't believe such rashness, even yours.
It *is* a joke!

HELEN
The President loves to jest.

LUCY
Yes, Mrs. Scopes, he humors anyone.
The world has wondered from what reservoir
so much exuberance can bubble up.

HYDE
That's not a mystery, woman; for the more
the world affronts my sensibility,
the more life reconciles me to the grave.
Adversity should wrench a stoic man
to joyous optimism: trouble blesses;
it's irritation that brings forth the pearl.
A man ought to be cheerful, since the worst
may never happen, our vast deficits
never drive Secretary Gainsborough to resign,
or me to give up any second term,
or you, dear Lucy, to divorce your spouse.

(LUCY rises.)

LUCY
After that, you must all excuse me, please.
I have a headache, and should like to sleep.

HYDE
Yes, certainly, my dear. You get some rest.
Would you like one of Dr. La Brea's drugs?

LUCY
I've drugs enough already, thanks to him.

(LUCY goes out.)

LA BREA
That was not well considered, Mr. Hyde.
As a physician, I deplore that you

LA BREA (Continued)
should upset the First Lady with a gibe!

HYDE
I stand rebuked. And plainly I've struck mute
Judge Harkins with my sudden nomination
of her to the Supreme Court. There still remains
the assembled Senate to confirm the choice.
It seems to take most people's breaths away.
Only the widow looks at all serene.

FRANCES
She hopes to be acquitted and go free.

HYDE
She's free already, Frances. Aren't you, Helen?

HELEN
Very. But not acquitted. Her Honor means
that in those weeks after my husband's death,
when seemingly I vanished into air,
I was in her backwater Bryan County,
a rural district, where I taught school children
the implications of the Modern Deal.
For that they've charged me with corrupting youth.
I'm out on bail now, but I must stand trial
soon in her courthouse.

FRANCES
                Mrs. Scopes has taught
her fifth grade pupils at the Bryan School
the economics of your Modern Deal.
One of the children's parents got upset,
and his attorney filed an action based
on an old statute that forbids the schools
to teach immoral or licentious doctrines.
The suit accuses Mrs. Scopes of preaching
a prurient theory: disrespect of money;
of teaching children an extravagance

FRANCES (Continued)
that makes men monkeys on a spending spree.
The lawsuit charges, Mr. President,
that your idea of deficit financed
by greenbacks isn't fit to teach the young.
The case already stirs some local talk.
I can't believe you didn't know of it.

HYDE
This *is* the first I've heard about the case.
How dogmatism makes the world go round,
and with hot air will always fill a vacuum!
Frances, your resignation from the Cabinet
may yet turn out a blessing in disguise.
Helen, I'm glad of this; I think I'm glad.
Your trial will surely test the Modern Deal
for constitutionality in law.
Nothing would suit me better than to try
the issue in Judge Harkins' country courthouse.

FRANCES
The statute might prove constitutional.

HYDE
No, not unless we stripped the truth away
of former friendship. Why, the greenback bills
were practically your own idea. Look, Frances,

(HYDE produces a bill from his pocket.)

at the design here; this is like an icon
for drawing worshipers to stand and rally.
My portrait in itself compels respect.
It shows my features unimpeachably.
Notice the noble brow, the honest profile.
Is that firm jaw unconstitutional?
And mind you, that's not even my good side.

FRANCES

I never should have come here, friends or not;
I never should have come.

HYDE

I'm glad you did.
Of course it was my wife's suggestion, Frances.

FRANCES

So I was told; but you had better call me
Judge Harkins, whether I'm confirmed or not
for the appointment. This is not a joke.
If I serve on the Bench, I'll jettison
our friendship sooner than play rubber stamp,
mangle the Constitution, act a puppet,
or drop the Court in any crony's pocket.
My entrails and my very heart will be
the robe and gavel, Frances then no more.
If you expect the Scopes trial to presage
my future rulings on the Modern Deal,
from Washington you'd better send some lawyers
to argue out the case on its own merits,
or else withdraw my nomination now.

LA BREA

At some cost to the President's prestige.
He has already announced your Honor's name.
You surely owe him something for the bribe.

FRANCES

For shame! This comes of being too cynical.

LA BREA

Madam, no one can be too cynical.
The papers chitter that in all the world
only a dozen men have understood
the President's new economic theory.
I'm not among them, nor, it seems, will be
any fifth graders of the Bryan School.

LA BREA (Continued)
Your Honor talks as cynically as I.

FRANCES
Then I will take my leave. Good day to you.

HELEN
Before you go, Judge Harkins, may I have
a word with you in private?

FRANCES
Very well.
President Hyde, Dr. La Brea, farewell.

(Exit FRANCES with HELEN.)

LA BREA
You look dashed, Hyde. Is this good news or bad?
As your chief backer, I should like to know.

HYDE
Frances was always honest, I admit.
Her nomination may miscarry us,
and the Supreme Court rule our nostrums out,
which means good night then to the Modern Deal.
But we haven't reached that stroke of midnight yet!
Nor even finished my initial term
in office, which has several months to go.
You promised four years, and a second term!

LA BREA
Provided you complied with our agreement:
a contract you've neglected for a while.
In the old days, my friend, I might have waited
upon the deadline, or extended it.
But on Black Thursday Halloween we struck
a bargain urgent for us both to honor.
It hasn't happened, and what you owe to me
on business principles I will collect.

HYDE

No ordinary business made us shut
the den door on your other guests, to talk
of politics alone before the fire.
To clinch the bargain we shook hands upon
a lightning bolt, and heard the radio
which had throughout the evening beamed band music
from a penthouse break off its scheduled broadcast,
and flash official-sounding bulletins
of strange invaders coming to the earth
from Mars in spaceships; beings, who were to us
as alien as the mountains of the moon,
had landed on the Stock Exchange, usurped
the markets, rigged investments, stocks and bonds,
and all Fort Knox's gold debased to lead.
In spite of all disclaimers, panic surged!
Wall Street thrashed wildly selling through the hours.
Nothing could stem the frenzied human rush
of telephoning brokers to unload
their holdings lock and stock, as Halloween
became a frantic scramble by the guests
to doff their costumes, in a fervid lunge
at disinvestment. Back and forth their fears
flitted like rabid bats. The Market downed
dozens of ruined investors, many of whom
leapt from high windows with their out-turned pockets
flapping like futile wings down to the pavements.
The country itself plummeted to sidewalks.
Banks failed, production sank, investment too.
Depression like a devil's tarpaulin
settled on people, trade, hope, everything.
By that I got elected, by your help.

LA BREA

And by that program on the radio
that frightened listeners to hysteria
in crying "Wolf!" which started the collapse.
You surely see no supernatural arts
brought down the system. You're a man of science!

27

HYDE

By no coincidence, but for my soul,
you made me President. You may belittle
our metaphysical collaboration,
but I consider, Doctor, it was you
who stepped me from the ranks of moral men,
as if the joker, or the jack of hearts
might step forth living from a deck of cards
as villainy personified. That's me.
You ought to humor me, and make a threat
of real damnation, and do it in earnest.

LA BREA

Confound it, Hyde, I *am* in earnest now!
Oh, very well then: play it any way;
go on and personalize the whole affair
in moral terms, with me the Prince of Darkness.
Only quit trying to market me your soul.
I'd sooner buy the Brooklyn Bridge from you.

HYDE

But that's the whole point! Humor me at least,
and say the words as if you really meant them.

LA BREA

All right, and so I do, my friend. All right.
A lingering damnation for the asking
is what you'll get from me. You ask for it.

HYDE

I don't have all the contract promised me.
Helen of Troy you never did deliver.

LA BREA

You mean the widow Scopes. Well, try her harder.
But this is quite romantic of you, Hyde.
Love surely proves what a good man you are.

HYDE

I never was and never will be good.

LA BREA

You are, you are; but also you craved power.
So for the past four years I've financed you
to steer the state, though as it happens, Hyde,
although depression lingers, yet it never
worsens because of you, and I suspect
that all your rhetoric of wickedness,
or anyway ambition, only hides
a most unhealthy craving to do good.

HYDE

Good, good. Just now you're talking like a devil
such rotten nonsense! I don't even know
what goodness is. What is good? You tell me.

LA BREA

A lack of evil, just as truth consists
only of the absence of falsehood and lies.
What you call good is something negative,
only the opposite of positive evil,
a vacuum where one's wickedness should be.

HYDE

I know I'm wicked.

LA BREA

From the first you've had
always some talk of balancing the budget;
and then compassion hiring Boris Wells,
when all the country blamed him for the crash.

HYDE

It was hypocrisy and platitudes
to win me some political support.

LA BREA

Please, no excuses, Mr. President.

HYDE

I don't think my performance falls so short.

LA BREA

In this world, evil is what gets things done.
In that respect, Hyde, you don't measure up.

HYDE

Rome didn't fall in just a single day.
The possibilities are diabolic!
The Modern Deal I've launched aims to debauch
the country into spending that corrupts
its currency and morals, spreading wide
festering insolvency, and by the debts
that heap on its descendants, will ensure
the country, like a mammoth, soon must sink
into a permafrost that never thaws.
When that day dawns, this present slump will seem
only a bracing bout of autumn weather
that stiffens virtue, even if depressing
men's pocketbooks. Then I expect a change:
a winter blasting every hope of picnic,
summer's grasshopper skidding the last weed
down from its optimism; winter born,
a new ice age, as chilled as human hearts,
where only a primitive invertebrate
might find the warmth to thaw and live again.
The loss of income, causing penury,
will rust the social hinges, and drive men
into a leaping of the moral fences,
and every jump bankrupt a character.
In tardy households, cuckoo clocks will cry
"Balance the budget!" while jobless men trudge
from door to door as nomads seeking work
to earn some spending money, lest they starve
on roots and handouts. Structures that endure
through business failures never will survive
an irresponsibility in conduct,
so I've led voters on a spending spree;

HYDE (Continued)
I've lit a grinning pumpkin in their night
to snuff out every sense of thrift and prudence,
so profligacy seems a commonplace,
greed swells above laws, and the budget ruptures.
Of course the demagogues will warp elections.
For people entertain the greatest lies
with the most credit; fools never suspect
villainy from a pillar of the state.
They'd rather sink their doubts in platitudes
that never solved a thing, all piety.
Why, I would bet the jawbone of an ass
against a thousand men, they lap it up.
Dr. La Brea, give my hypocrisy
a place to stand on, and I will move the earth.

LA BREA
That's wonderful, my friend, magnificent!
Your second term is coming. Fire fights fire,
Satan casts Satan out, bad dollars drive
good dollars down. When none is worth a dime,
the country will be lost. Then mine, all mine!

(HELEN returns.)

Madam, I leave you to the President.
I must go pull strings with the other party!

(LA BREA hurries out.)

HYDE
Helen, I rather wonder if your case
is something better settled out of court.

HELEN
My case is built on my late husband's plane,
which you built also, as your program paid
for its development. You have made me
forever grateful, Mr. President,

HELEN (Continued)

for so much goodness.

HYDE

            Oh, don't talk of goodness.
Don't think me good! The only thing I fear
is goodness, or having some good to lose.

HELEN

Not talk of goodness? I don't understand.

HYDE

Nearly four Halloweens ago occurred
a national masquerade for certain parties
in garb betokening their main investments.
I dressed as Uncle Sam in stars and stripes,
which signified my presidential aims,
as other guests wore costumes themed as well.
Some with banking shares wore top hats and tails;
two agricultural speculators walked
as barefoot boys beneath their hats of straw;
a railway magnate sported overalls;
a mining mogul bore a lantern, pick,
and carried a canary in a cage.
Dr. La Brea, was also there, our host,
in the attire of Mephistopheles.
And there was you.

HELEN

            I daresay I was there,
without an invitation or my husband:
a friend of mine and I just crashed the gate.

HYDE

We met each other on that night of nights.
To speak more bluntly, madam, there was set
a destiny that still is incomplete.

HELEN

I have to wonder, sir. To me a party
always would beckon me to heaven borne
on manic wings, wild in a little room,
a kitchen even, talkative and festive,
too flirty for my husband who was furious.
In my high spirits those days I'd frolic, ride
on taxi roofs, plunge into plaza fountains,
spray money shopping, on yachts float away
whole afternoons with friends, till the sun sank.
At dusk speakeasies opened. Then we'd drink
champagne from our shoes, gamble in casinos,
and dance the evenings full to overflowing,
and pour them into all-night parties. Dawns
we stole the cream off what the milkman left.

HYDE

The boom days of youth on its hellish fling.
It was a decade of such costume parties.
We all miss them, except perhaps my Lucy.

HELEN

Soon our extravagance required more money,
so Hector set about designing aircraft,
for a great airplane was a pretty toy
for rich investors. To drum up their interest
at masquerades, I'd often dramatize
the new design by dressing in the garb
of female pilot. Parties were my way
of dragging Hector from his blueprint desk.
Because I loved to vamp the other men,
he had to come out on the town with me.
By the time he'd completed his design,
poor Hector was a drunkard due to me.
He should've loathed the ground I walk upon!

HYDE

How different from my own reaction, Helen!
Or Mrs. Scopes, if I may call you that.

HYDE (Continued)
I never could resist a married woman.
Your wedded status dazzled me, and swept
away my judgement. All that night I joked
about the next election, called myself
a politician, grubbed in common clay;
and yet you reared my interests heavenward.
Yes, you gave inspiration. In your raiment
you crowned the parallel, and seemed to make
Helen of Troy alive down to her sandals.
You wore a diversely colored garment, hued
in part as yellow as a crocus flower,
but also amber, wheat and numerous browns,
with green of course ensnared in everything.
Your cape was purple stitched with moon and stars,
and in your hair a kind of garland grew
with classic connotations. At your brow
appeared a band inscribed with lunar disks
borne up by serpents, or just wavy lines
that maybe symbolized the furrowed earth.
Some blades of corn stood bowed to either side
of yet another emblem of the moon.
I think the moon; but I forget the rest.
Oh, in one hand you held a cup of gold.

HELEN
I sound like quite an agricultural dish.
Helen of Troy you thought?

HYDE
                    The Doctor told me
that the resemblance wasn't only fancied,
but that the whole election, and your person,
hung in the balance if our bargain held,
and so I undertook to fund the plane
designed by your then husband; I approached you.

HELEN
Not me. I know that woman you describe

HELEN (Continued)
who wasn't me that evening. Someone else.

HYDE
You must be joking!

HELEN
I assure you, no.
She—my friend—told me of it afterwards.

HYDE
But that's my whole conception of the evening!
Another woman in a different guise?

HELEN
Dressed just as you described, while I had on
an aviatrix costume for the party.
Toward her I saw you gliding with your hand
up high, just like a shark's fin cutting through
the water of the other guests to reach her,
and doing so you bowed and mimed a whimsy,
which later she explained to me: your wrist
by strings unseen was bringing her the moon,
which, bowing, you presented as a gift.
No angler ever cast a stranger line.

HYDE
The mountain somehow had to come to you.
But now my head is spinning. That was someone else?

HELEN
Yes.

HYDE
Really, she wasn't you?

HELEN
Not me at all.

HYDE

Well, how exceedingly inept I've been
in my addresses! I must have been drunk
on an unearthly liquor! Was I drunk?

HELEN

I daresay your attention didn't pierce
beyond appearances, and then one comes
upon no mirror of the soul at all,
but only mere attire of no account,
and finds the commonest mole a subtle decoy
misleading the attention. Love gets fixed
on surfaces no deeper than the skin.
To find the truth a man of wisdom delves
beneath apparel. What that is may vary.
Oh, you needn't apologize to me.
The woman fascinated you that year;
she was my predecessor in our movement.
This year is my turn. So great is the value
of our attire the woman doesn't matter
who puts it on. Each wears it in her time.

HYDE

By movement you must mean political.

HELEN

I do. And now I want to strike a bargain
for your compliance.

HYDE

            But I *have* complied.
I've financed building of your husband's plane
with the economy still smashed to earth,
and with investment funds for other aircraft
evaporated snowflakes on a spit.
My Modern Deal, Helen, has means to launch
a thousand of the ships your spouse designed.
I won't deny that you gave me the motive
for such investment; but you've not responded

HYDE (Continued)
with any grateful passion. To your movement
I think I've given practically the moon
for nothing in return.

HELEN
                    You've given nothing.
Oh, Mr. President, beware the moon,
a mistress that in unexpected ways
will disappoint you. I was not the woman
you met on Halloween four years ago.
To build my husband's plane may ease my conscience;
to put my picture on your currency
might flatter vanity; but these are nothings.
Suppose I want the wilderness and moon.

HYDE
Now certainly those aren't subcabinet posts.

HELEN
I'm mascot to a conservation lobby.
We want political consideration.

HYDE
A conservation lobby!

HELEN
                    Our White Tower
works to preserve the unspoiled wilderness
of unpolluted streams, the unbowed timber
that grows proud parallels up mountainsides,
the nurturing territory that supports
the very humans now who threaten it
with their steamrolling growth. We want to keep
your Modern Deal from flourishing too far.
None of the new air crews must ever land
with a defiling cargo on the moon,
or in the wilderness. This we propose.
To tread the gray dust of a moon, men pile

HELEN (Continued)

pollution on a pyramiding debt.
Our members toil to save the natural world
whose logo is the moon. They yearly choose
somebody to personify the wild
in gown and powder, as you now perceive
my predecessor wore that fateful evening
the emblem of our movement. I embody
the same thing this year. People have to learn
not just the gifts of nature, nature too.
The very harvest of the earth depends
on nature's bounty; so we picture her
as a manifold white goddess who can take
the outline of a crane in flight, an owl
or albatross, albino sow or mare;
the mistress, mother, hag: the triple muse
the ancient druids worshipped in their groves.
She had a face as white as leprosy,
as life-in-death; her skin the sheet of death,
the threefold goddess of the moon.

HYDE

                                    Good heavens!
You say my program threatens wilderness,
yet you agreed to going on with it.
We built your husband's aircraft, sent it up!

HELEN

Yes, and I drove my husband to the sky:
I threatened that unless he flew the ocean,
I'd fly myself to Europe and divorce him.
So up flew Hector solo. He'd imbibed
a drink or two beforehand to support
his courage, and that must have caused his crash.

HYDE

You tempted him to that, no mercy?

HELEN

                    None.
The witch in me delights to play with fire,
and fan the flames to set them burning higher.
By my enticing Hector played the hero,
and that bravado surely cost his life.

HYDE

Lucy at least never tried poisoning me!
Oh, I'd divorce her now, if I could kiss
good-by to reëlection. What to do?
The oddest lobbyist that I ever met.
You're irresistible! You ought to be
my Secretary of the Wilderness.
Between the dark and light you've struck my soul
with inspiration, and a playfulness
that tips the scales between some mighty forces.

HELEN

Do I know any of these mighty forces?
I have a certain curiosity,
though you haven't believed a word of mine.

HYDE

I do. I always took you for a goddess,
and I grant any concept you propose
as revelation, anything at all.
My mind's an airstrip paved for new ideas
to land on; cratered deep and battered by them.
Yet how I wish we'd settle out of court!
I wish your testimony as my mistress
were inadmissible in court of law!
I'll come to earth now, Helen, offer you
my hand in partnership on bendèd knee.

        (HYDE drops to one knee. LUCY enters with a suitcase,
        and observes.)

Do you accept my suit?

HELEN

This is an error, Mr. President.
What would the public think of this behavior?

HYDE

As normal Cabinet manners, madam: look
how I abase myself, your suppliant
that we might plead insanity in court.
Helen, I wish your trial might never happen!
For even if we win, some may accuse
Frances of bias favoring a friend;
so even with acquittal, we might gain
only a pittance. Let us strike a bargain.
I'll make the ultimate proposal now:
I offer you our party's nomination
as my Vice-presidential running mate.

LUCY

You have a mate already, Reynard. Stand up.

(HE rises.)

HYDE

Lucy! I thought you took a sleeping pill.
I've only just now offered Mrs. Scopes
a place beside me on the party ticket.

LUCY

So I observed.

HYDE

      And, Helen: I won't ask for
any immediate answer to my offer.
You take your time to think it over first.

(HE takes out of his pocket and hands HELEN a card.)

This card has the phone number and address
of that renowned defender of lost causes:

HYDE (Continued)
Oliver Barrell. He may help the case.

HELEN
Mrs. Hyde, you look dressed about to travel.
On your return I think we ought to talk.

LUCY
We've nothing to talk over, Mrs. Scopes.
I probably shall not be coming back.

HELEN
With your permission, madam, then I'll bid
good-by to President Hyde . . .

(HELEN kisses HYDE.)

HYDE
Oh, Helen, I would like to lie with you!

HELEN
Well, I think you've been lying all along.

(SHE leaves.)

HYDE
Why the suitcase and the handbag, Lucy?
Where are you going, never to return?
If you intend to quit me, Waldo Waldo's
the man you want.

LUCY
          Oh, that's a cruel remark.
I should have walked out on you long ago.
In everything, you speak with double meanings.

HYDE
I hope so, dearest, as I have become
a politician facing reëlection.

LUCY

I'm leaving, John; it's time we were divorced.

HYDE

You have no grounds to sue me for divorce!

LUCY

Your attachment to your paramour
blazons a separate world; so I should seek
a better situation for myself.
Nothing has ever really bound me here,
except my own devotion, which kept locked
a door to which I myself held the key,
though leaving you seemed more than I could bear.
To think how blind I've been! I see at last
my life with you as a revolving door
that I can pass through freely. John: I leave
you to your mistress and experiments,
your drug-dispensing Doctor and his pills,
your bathtub arias, everything, to catch
a streamliner out to Reno, and divorce.
I've called a cab already. I can stay
at some hotel until my train departs.

HYDE

Wait, Lucy! Things today are not that simple.
I didn't want to mention this before,

(HE doubles over, almost out of sight behind his desk.)

but I have shooting pains that come and go.
Like there!—Just now! Oh, Lucy, through my heart

(The phone rings.)

there hardly throbs a pulse. Listen to the phone
ringing for you—I'll warrant it's for you!

(His hand shoots up and takes the phone. HYDE stands. LUCY pauses.)

HYDE (Continued)
Hello. One moment, dear. Hello . . .
Isn't there anybody on the line?
Whose breathing do I hear? Is someone there?

LUCY
It must be just another crank who's called.
I'll leave you to it, John, and say good-by
to your unbroken heart. You have no heart.

HYDE
Another minute, Lucy, just a minute!
This is important; try to understand
my situation. If I lose the crank vote
I could lose the election. Someone's there!

(LUCY goes out.)

Gone.
My friend, whoever you may be, I trust
your heavy breathing means my words have moved you.
Give me your name at least, and we'll discuss
granting support of your peculiar pastime.

(Enter LA BREA with BOSKY.)

What madness! Everybody! Gentlemen,
come in: my wife found that's an open door.

(HYDE slams down the receiver.)

Ah, just in time, erring but mortal, comes
my Treasury agent. Mr. Bosky, welcome!
And, Doctor, you again? You can't imagine
how gladly my heart leaps that you should keep
our four o'clock appointment. Do come in.
Sit down. No need to stand on ceremony.

LA BREA

Better that you sit, Mr. President,
because the Agent and I bring report
of a catastrophe.

HYDE

What do you mean?
Surely not that our Treasury Secretary
Gainsborough has finally turned from words to deeds.
He's threatened resignation times enough.

LA BREA

No, he admits your gift of Midas, Hyde,
because some unexpected profits have
suddenly now emerged perplexing him.
Any accountant knows that spending money
makes money disappear. Yet now it seems
that Treasury revenues are on the rise;
the more prodigiously the Treasury spends
away the dollars, more the dollars breed
as if our spending multiplied our funds,
for every dollar government doles out
returns in taxes triple that amount!
It's a spread-eagled heresy, a dream
of profit utter rubbish on our books.
Pages that should show red are black with profit!
So Mr. Bosky has explained to me.

HYDE

We show an actual profit, do you say?

BOSKY

To put it bluntly, Mr. President,
this comes of printing bills backed up by nothing.
My acid test has always been hard facts.
An ass would rather munch on straw than gold;
a man should sink his teeth in what is real,
weigh every dime, prove every nickel, bite
the Indian till he yelps. You can't make money

BOSKY (Continued)
of paper promises and IOU's
without some form of metal backing it,
though saying so makes me sound like a dentist.

HYDE
Yes, yes, the government lacked ore to base
denominated script on gold and silver;
we might as well have sought the sun and moon.
If only someone had found new gold mines!
I share your worry, and I've braced myself
against calamity, tossed nights, and wandered
in corridors, with deep foreboding felt
that the bare bones of my abstract idea
might be eclipsed by the flesh of this world.
The worst that happened can be nothing worse
than I've imagined. Now you say a profit!
A profit, Agent Bosky, no mistake?

BOSKY
Sir, no mistake.

LA BREA
Such happy tidings, Hyde.

HYDE
Is this a dream of Michelson and Morley
whose lightning never found a resting place?
or the Klein bottle that can release a genie
by popping inside out? or Möbius strip
where creeps an upright beetle upside down?
or Zeno's bow whose arrows through midpoints
shot take forever never to hit home?
The Modern Deal by debt can net a profit?
Of course a modern universe curves back
upon itself, warping the parallels
the straightest way, to meet themselves.
But money is traditional and old—
or is that wrong? I feel a little sick!

HYDE (Continued)
Despite the expert advice that I defied,
so necessary seemed it to defy
expert advice, a profit you report?

LA BREA
You're starting to repeat yourself, my friend.

BOSKY
Before you gentlemen decide to take
these latest revenues at their face value,
remember that the profit must be fake.

HYDE
Yes!
Fake would make it flattering news indeed!

BOSKY
I never flatter, Mr. President.
Your Modern Deal provided printing presses
for paper money letting people buy
real merchandise; except they only pay
with currency too slippery to be true.
Now someone else has aped the government,
and started minting greenbacks for their gain.
There is a counterfeiting ring at work.

HYDE
Ah, counterfeiting rather! I commend
your bluntness telling me unvarnished fact
about the unhappy truth of bogus profits,
which news I welcome better late than never.
Well: let's track down and apprehend the culprits
who do the forging.

BOSKY
                    And the plates employed.

HYDE
Yes, but work circumspectly; take no chances.
After the panic of four years ago,
we wouldn't want another on our hands.

LA BREA
We wouldn't want the news to leak out yet.

BOSKY
What are you dreaming, Doctor? Not a word
about this fiasco ever should be aired,
for everybody knows that counterfeiting
threatens the fabric of society.

LA BREA
So we must shut the forgers down.

BOSKY
                              Yes, sir.

HYDE
This moment, Agent Bosky, have you any
examples of sham bills we might inspect?

BOSKY
No, Mr. President.

HYDE
                    Ah.

BOSKY
                              Not as yet.

HYDE
Alas, then that makes matters rather awkward.

BOSKY
The forgeries resemble genuine cash
so closely any telling them apart
calls for an expert taking extra time

BOSKY (Continued)
to nail down definitely which is which.

HYDE
Can they be so alike, or maybe even
identical?—Or are you flattering me
that no material counterfeit exists?

BOSKY
Except they show up by their copious flow
in all directions. They exist all right.

HYDE
Ah, yes, quite so. The proof is indirect.

BOSKY
This very moment we have agents keeping
under surveillance in the District here
a certain warehouse owned by Herring Storage,
one of a chain of places we suspect
of counterfeiting. There we may find plates.

HYDE
Good Lord!

LA BREA
You, Mr. President, look rather stunned.

HYDE
Only imagine! With not a folding note
in evidence, we have no proof at all
that any counterfeiting has occurred.
But there I go again feeding my hopes
without a reason. Agent Bosky, thank you
for your reporting of this money crime,
and of that house of ill repute now owned
by Herring Storage. I, too, have received
reports of lavish tax receipts from there.
Good work: keep on with your investigation.

BOSKY

I'll double all our stakeouts night and day,
and get a warrant, sir, to raid the place.

HYDE

No, best you wait a while, and keep the house
under surveillance till you hear from me.
Let's give those forgers lots of rope. Good luck!

BOSKY

Yes, sir.

HYDE

And act alone!

(BOSKY leaves. HYDE collapses in a chair.)

I can't believe it!

LA BREA

Believe what, Hyde? What are you fussing over?

HYDE

To pieces I can feel my heart now pounding!

LA BREA

Pounding for what, man? Pounding what about!

HYDE

Oh, Doctor, Doctor, you must surely see
the suspect revenues are genuine:
no forgeries exist! no ring exists!
no counterfeit at all! My program works!
I choke to say it, but the Modern Deal
belies the scam that I began in jest,
and unexpectedly it flourishes!

LA BREA

Flourishing you call it! Pull yourself

together, man. Quit ranting and explain
your meaning that no counterfeit exists.
That Agent says it does, and figures show
anomalous revenue that otherwise
looks inexplicable. Or is this just
more bragging indirectly of your goodness?

(Abruptly HYDE leaps again to his feet in denial.)

HYDE

There's not in me even a grain of good!
I've passed myself off as an elder statesman;
I've violated monetary law;
I've tempted people to a spending spree
that sapped their prudence; I've made public thrift
past history in a binge that's rid the country
of parsimonious morals, wholly blown
tradition to the backside of the moon
like pollen from my hand. I've stretched so wide
the budget to the verge it should've ruptured,
except my alchemy has somehow backfired!
Mad, ponderable phenomena have turned
my bogus dollars into solid gold,
my airy paradoxes into sense,
my falsehoods woven into verities
that terrify my hairs to stand on end.
La Brea, like a proper fiend, I lied
about my program, focused all my sight
on a deception that turned out right.
My spending program boomerangs! It prospers!
Oh, in this world lurks more than meets the eye.
Things aren't as we see them; nor do we see
ourselves aright; for I, who never swerved
even from murder, hit a notion fit
more for a benefactor than a villain!
Only the man I was was counterfeit.
What does that make me, Doctor? Now reformed?
I never dreamt the truth might grow

HYDE (Continued)
into one's heart a root that splits the stone.
Why, all this time my devil was an angel,
and I, John Hyde, have been the age's fool!
Doctor, I don't feel quite myself today.

(HE slumps into a chair.)

LA BREA
Then lie here till the stroke of midnight puts you
out of your misery! You wretched weather vane,
by your incompetence you've bungled all
that we shook hands on! You've backslid and blundered
back to a prosperity of happy days!
I wanted the depression strung along
so we might have some monetary chaos,
but you had to corrupt the home and hearth,
warp everybody's morals, which renders them
not human anymore, and not so evil.
Jack Hyde, the mastermind and evil genius,
my partner to the limits of the known world!
My expert versed in economic theory!

HYDE
I did the worst that anyone could dream.

LA BREA
Your worst is wearing goodness like a collar!
You always flirted with philanthropy.
Next you'll tip over prams, or on the street
steal widows' purses, or grandmothers' coins!

HYDE
I do have malice, nine-tenths me lies below
the surface hidden as an iceberg's bulk.
Discovering counterfeit will prove me wicked.

LA BREA
But you just said no counterfeit exists!

(HYDE leaps to his feet.)

HYDE

And you've just heard how fondly Bosky dreams
of its existence, and by evidence
that we can plant ourselves for him to find,
our Agent can be vindicated yet.
Why, I could pinpoint on a map for you
hundreds of houses like the Herring warehouse
where we might lay a bait of spurious clues
to set on fire, so raising an alarm
will bring the law to sift the smoking rubble
for evidence of forging in the ashes.
The embers of suspicions there will glow,
will flare and kindle, blaze in fiscal panic.
A happy prospect, Doctor. Trust to arson,
and I'll nip this recovery in the bud.

LA BREA

Then do it, Hyde. Resort to anything.
So desperate this last scheme might even work.
You may have six days for it.

HYDE

                    Only six!

LA BREA

By close of business, at the stroke of twelve,
only a week from now, I'll find you here.

(LA BREA leaves, HYDE follows.)

<u>END OF SCENE 2</u>

SCENE 3

An insane asylum. WALDO enters in a wheel chair pushed by
DAISY. SHE stops and takes from her pocket a bottle and spoon.

DAISY

Here you go, Waldo, time for medicine!

WALDO

I hate the medicine you make me take
in this asylum, and I hate this place.
I've had enough of it here; I want out.

DAISY

Oh, no. You'll have to stay in Shady Corners
until the Doctor says you're well again.
Obey the rules and take your medicine
like a good patient. Here we have your dose.

(SHE offers the medicine.)

Take it, and on the radio we can hear
the broadcast of the trial of Mrs. Scopes.

WALDO

I never want to listen to the trial
when everybody knows that no one has
responsibility for his own self,
but only for the influence that he has
on someone else. The President I blame
for my attack on him against my will
that went so wrong. Before I squeezed the trigger,
my whole life flashed a movie through my mind,
with my own name not even in the credits!

DAISY

That gives a person lots to brood about.

WALDO

The Doctor tells me no one has a self
beneath his layers that just peel away.
To find my real identity, I tried
to shoot the President against my will.
I finally know that, now that I've been cured.

DAISY

Well, not quite cured; but soon you'll be yourself,
if you'll just take your medicine.

WALDO

                                    No, thanks.

DAISY

Oh, do coöperate. Today's your birthday,
and someone even baked a cake for you,
and left a present at the lobby desk
wrapped in a ribbon. You can open it
in celebration. You can also view
your portrait that I finished yesterday.
But first you have to take your daily dose.

                    (LA BREA comes in.)

WALDO

I like surprises; I hate medicine.
Give me a cake and file; forget the pills.

LA BREA

Good afternoon, Nurse Lyons.
Do you remember me: Lamont La Brea?

DAISY

Oh, yes! Waldo, this is Dr. La Brea,
the founder of the sanitarium.

LA BREA

Thanks to some large donations, Mr. Waldo,

LA BREA (Continued)
we'll have you up and running very soon.
Someday men may grow salads on the seas
to feed the hungry, colonize the moon,
or rehabilitate the thieves and muggers,
if not their victims, since we're only human.
Meantime our staff does its imperfect best.
Here doctors, nurses, guards and inmates, all
would influence you for your own benefit.

WALDO
Oh, anyone can influence me, but me.

DAISY
Waldo refuses to take medicine
his therapy requires. He's being bad.

WALDO
Why, even on my birthday, down my throat
thrust the do-gooders pills on me their victim.

DAISY
Today's his birthday. Waldo wants a gift,

LA BREA
Then leave your patient tête-à-tête with me,
and I may get him to coöperate.
Behind the lobby desk, nurse, you will find
a gift to Waldo someone left today.
Go bring it here, please. I've here medicine

(HE exhibits a spoon and bottle.)

prescribed you, Waldo, for your peristalsis.

(DAISY goes out. LA BREA pours syrup into the spoon.)

And in this spoon, friend, is a treat for you,
if now you'll only open wide your mouth.

(WALDO turns away his face.)

LA BREA (Continued)
Don't turn away there! Look me in the eyes!

WALDO
So you can hypnotize me? No, I won't.

LA BREA
And I say you shall do it. Look at me!
If it demands some forcing, look you will.

(With one black-gloved hand, LA BREA forces WALDO's head around.)

Open you mouth, and wide. You're in my power!

(WALDO swallows the medicine.)

Yes, down it went, and did it taste so bad?
Congratulations, Waldo. You were brave,
and we can celebrate your birthday now.

(DAISY brings on a tray a package to WALDO.)

Your present, Waldo, and a happy birthday!
Although the package doesn't say from whom.

LA BREA
But decorated festively enough
for a special Saturday tonight.
There's certainly as well a cake to come,
and I'd also like to witness the unwrapping,
but duty calls. Nurse, walk me to the lobby.
There's something special I must say to you.
It will take but a minute.

DAISY
All right, Doctor.

DAISY (Continued)
Then, Waldo, you must not unwrap your gift
till I come back, and with me bring the cake.

(Exit DAISY.)

LA BREA
A couple weeks ago, I heard you clipped
a handgun coupon from a magazine,
and mailed it to receive a free home trial
of thirty days. Your parcel has arrived.
You face a showdown with the President.
He defies you to shoot it out with him
at dusk on Main Street, if you're man enough.

WALDO
I'm man to show him up at any showdown.
I'd face him, but I haven't got a gun.

LA BREA
Nor outdoor clothing; but you'll soon have both.
Only don't mention weapons to the nurse.
And don't forget, Waldo, to make a wish.

(LA BREA goes out. WALDO fingers the package.)

WALDO
He tried to hypnotize me, but so great
is my will power he failed, for I'm the master!—
Force is my last resort, but let me peek
beneath the wrapping. Nurse will never know.

(HE starts to unwrap the gift.)

When she returns, my cunning will pretend
to be surprised. Off with your wrapping quick!

(Out of the opened package HE lifts a revolver.)

WALDO (Continued)

Ah!...

How did they ever guess my handgrip size!?
And the expense! They really shouldn't have!
It fits me perfect, and it's loaded too!

(HE aims the gun.)

I'm back in business, Mr. Hyde, with you.

(WALDO rises and steals out.)

END OF SCENE 3

SCENE 4

Again a White House office. Through different doors HELEN and LUCY enter. LUCY carries a suitcase; HELEN wears a white dress.

LUCY

You!
I leave the house, and you install yourself
as my replacement. I expected that.

HELEN

Please don't misunderstand my being here
for any subterfuge, my dear First Lady—
if so I may address you.

LUCY

               Oh, indeed;
despite my fine intention to divorce
I've circled back to where I started out,
and still am Mrs. Hyde right now as was,
which you apparently have guessed already.
I'm not divorced. It came into my mind
how advantageous more than otherwise
if I continued in my role of wife.
Really John's reëlection hopes depend
upon avoiding all domestic scandal,
and that almost might render him my hostage.

HELEN

You seem more independent than before,
and that is very reassuring, Madam.

LUCY

I still would like to get away from him.

HELEN

But never mind about that for the present.

LUCY

You sound much less astonished than myself.

HELEN

Your recent journey and return are news.
The stories in the paper make us wonder
whether your journey veered another way.

LUCY

So you've been reading of me in the press.

HELEN

Was your trip fruitful?

LUCY

You might say so—yes!
It brought illumination of a sort
so unexpected one can scarce imagine
that an experience in a railway coach
could have so much significance.

HELEN

Try me.

LUCY

I changed trains once midway, and caught the zephyr
that slowly from the station eased itself
from city on to outskirts, then to farmland,
toward wilderness, with speed increasing westward
the streaking zephyr swept me on its way
across the continent to be divorced.
Woodland gave way to prairie, that to mountains;
day turned to night, the sun went down, moon up.
The coaches clattered on.
I had the whole compartment to myself,
and brooded on my situation, felt
greatly abused; and through the window gazed
upon a wilderness of pristine rivers,
unsevered forests, single pines that blurred
by as they passed in view. The rhythmic sway
of train on track began to mesmerize
me into an unconsciousness or trance.

LUCY (Continued)
Soon I was just reflected in the window,
a ghostly witness that through glass observed
a world beyond any metropolis.
I wondered what a shame some progress is.
My husband's founding of prosperity
on asphalt seems to bode a world as spent
as my train ticket the conductor punched.
Out of my reverie, roused, up I rose
to quit the coach at the next station stop,
and from the platform caught a train bound home.

HELEN
Home-bound to haunt yourself?

LUCY
                              To haunt my husband
who often haunted me. Is that revenge?

HELEN
It's liberation. Lucy, you belong
within our movement for the wilderness,
where profligacy bodes mankind's undoing.
Yes! For the human species in its billions
scarcely abides the other animals,
or any limit to what we can extract
from the environment that fossils us.
Our group sees danger in your husband's program
of an untrammeled enterprise, world-wide,
that may extend even to outer space.
Your husband promises a higher sky
at a tremendous risk. The outer vacuum
is nothing but men's vacant dream to flee
to profligacy on a different world,
where they can live as wasteful as before;
but they'd fill up that new place, flee again,
and flee to further failure yet again,
orbiting things as threatening to themselves
as prehistoric mammals that evolved

HELEN (Continued)
horns curving round as aimed at their own skulls.

LUCY
Do all the members of your lobby go
about in powder looking deathly pale?

HELEN
This year they chose me to personify
the goddess; but it's not a powder, child;
rather a power we have to help control
metabolism and the flow of blood.

(LUCY sways as if dizzy.)

LUCY
Oh, I'm beginning now to wonder here.
You mean your cult has secret disciplines
to make one dizzy and control my thoughts?

(HELEN leads LUCY by the arm to a chair.)

HELEN
Only the personifier has such power—
but you should sit down—Yes, and trust to me.

(LUCY sits.)

Call it a secret technique, if you'd rather.

LUCY
I hardly can stand up or understand
your meanings now: I really do feel faint.

(LUCY leans forward in the chair and sinks to the floor.)

HELEN
For many reasons, Lucy, you should know
the White Tower movement that I represent

HELEN (Continued)
deplores the Modern Deal. We want to stem
mankind's mad march of progress, and we need
numbered among our members many friends
and active allies, possibly yourself.
We pity your position. We can see
how trodden down you are, and yet how blessed
with influence to exert if once you tried.

LUCY
I've tried escaping; even so I'm back,
and find you here. Where is my husband now?

HELEN
Out laying plots, I should imagine, madam.
But never mind his machinations yet.

LUCY
What do you want of me?

HELEN
                    A godsend's help.
Buttress your heart against unbridled growth
of the economy. Stay with your husband,
and try to loop some boundaries round the man.
He may live many years, and reach old age,
but by domestic pressure wear him down.
With help from you our movement will prevail.
Stay kneeling, Lucy. Let me have your hand.

(LUCY does.)

Keep faith with us, and that will see you through
the many possibilities there are
to keep a way of life distinct from death.
Do you accept my hand?

LUCY
                    Oh, I don't know—

LUCY (Continued)
Good heavens, madam, now you frighten me!
You talk as if the President might die!

HELEN
You want to sacrifice yourself for good,
and here's your opportunity: shun thoughts
of a divorce, no matter what provokes you.

LUCY
Even your sleeping in my husband's bed?

HELEN
He thrills to have a dangerous escapade,
and if it comes to that, nothing will help.

(HYDE comes in, cloaked, but throwing it off.)

LUCY
Is that you, John?

HYDE
                    That's what I ask myself.
To whom does my returning wife now stoop
more humbly than I knelt the day she left?
Lucy, what does it mean? Outside I saw
a new full moon illuminating night.
Have you returned to me? You're welcome home,
but no more conversation from the floor.
Do please stand up.

(Silence. LUCY rises.)

Well, Lucy, haven't you anything to say?

LUCY
Since Mrs. Scopes commanded me to share,
or give you up, I have just one condition.

HYDE
I'd give myself up, dear, if I could sound
as resolute as you do. I'd accept
any condition, living up to none.
You know my character and what it is.

(*LUCY goes to the door.*)

LUCY
I know exactly nothing.

HYDE
Lucy, wait!

LUCY
I've come to share your fate.

HYDE
What do you mean?

(*Exit LUCY.*)

Helen, there's something different with my wife.
She has returned, yet hardly seems the same.

HELEN
About your wife you may find something changed—

HYDE
If Lucy really has come back to me,
then she delivers me the married vote.
Divorce would damn my reëlection chances,
and yet I hardly care. She's lost to me.
No matter that, if only you repent
of going longer on as mourning widow
opposed to my advances. Yield to that.
Think of the President! Think of my office!

HELEN

Think of the infrastructure of your country.
On Monday I return to court to hear
Judge Harkins' ruling in my scapegoat trial.
You've got to halt the economic boom.

HYDE

I'm trying to halt it. If you only knew
how many different ways I'm trying to halt it!
My bad faith pledge has taken on a life
planted of greenbacks, where I nurtured desert.
The Modern Deal is generating profit!

HELEN

The profit will prove doubtful for the land,
and very nature; men best put away
dreams of untrammeled growth up to the stars.
Life's breeding bed is down here on the earth.

HYDE

Oh, now you're serious, trying to put me off
again, as always. You'll recede from me.
looking as pale as ever does the moon,
but not for loving me, as well I know.
I hoped you came here for the night, so white
with powders loathsome to me! I detest
disguises other people may put on.
This evening as a king of old I went
disguised among the people to inquire
the public's real opinion of my greenbacks.
I fathomed nothing. Someone followed me.
I lost him, and perhaps I lost myself.
playing the mountebank. My critics mock
that every man should criticize himself,
but in my circumstances that would be
unpatriotic. Hah! Now that's a joke.
If you refuse to spend the night with me,
Helen, you might at least smile at my jokes.

HELEN

You need a doctor; you're getting upset,
or even ill. I'll phone the Doctor—

HYDE

No!

A doctor diagnosed me long ago
for a deterioration of the heart,
and there was nothing he could do about it.
Free will and cause are like a two-faced god
of life and death; and life in me exists
within my own inherent character,
beyond excuses, and there's no beholder
can lever reasons of effect and cause
to make it otherwise. I'm not a pawn
of any explanation. What I did
I willed to do without an alibi.
To plead external fate forced me to crime
would rationalize to insignificance
my whole existence: I blame nothing on
the wide environment, the age, or stars.
This leopard loves his spots; so never fear
petty excuses grafting good on me
where no good ever grew. I've made my bed.

HELEN

And must lie in it.

HYDE

Will you join me there?

HELEN

Oh, yes; this is our final chance of it.

HYDE

I knew eventually it had to be,
in spite of all my cynicism, this.

HELEN

Forgive my mentioning it, but I should speak
first with your wife, for her permission, John.

HYDE

What!

HELEN

Don't look astonished at an etiquette
I find desirable in love affairs.
You needn't worry: Lucy half complies
already with the motions of the moon,
and she'll embrace our movement to the full
of humoring both of us. I'll come right back;
I promise not to disappoint you then.

(HELEN goes out.)

HYDE

How glorious, glorious! It seems sure today
my reëlection. What a strange foreplay.

(LA BREA enters twirling his cane.)

Dr. La Brea!

LA BREA

Mr. President,
the reckoning hour of midnight draws apace.
You have no hope of any more reprieves.
You've lost your campaign; payment now falls due,
and I've come to collect the debt you owe.

(LA BREA touches his cane to HYDE's chest. HYDE snatches it and
breaks it.)

HYDE

No, Doctor, blast it! Not till twelve o'clock
does anything expire. Wait till the time.

HYDE (Continued)
I'll see the planet damned before I yield
a moment early. I've come back tonight
expecting the last minute I'll escape.

LA BREA
On that it's no use counting: you were followed.

HYDE
That's just the sort of comment you let fall
before you disappear into the air.

(HE throws aside the two pieces of the broken cane.)

I know these tricks of yours; you come and go
pretending to know all. It's only bluff.

(BOSKY, panting, almost falls into the room.)

Get out!

BOSKY
Nobody leaves the premises.

HYDE
Is that you, Agent Bosky? Do come in.
Tonight I half-expected you might call
about that warehouse owned by Herrings.
Has something happened there?

BOSKY
Yes, Mr. President—I'm out of breath!
Something suspicious—I have to report.
All evening I've been staked outside the place.

HYDE
And then you dashed here gasping with the news.
So let me guess: the building's burning?

BOSKY

                                                      Yes,
flames flickered through a window; out the door
hurried an unfamiliar silhouette
into the darkness. The building blazed a moment,
and then went dark itself. When I got there
the fire had sputtered out and left a reek
in one room only, paraffin and smoke,
but nothing burning. From another room
went stumbling out-of-doors a second shadow
with outlined in his arms what I supposed
were counterfeiting plates snatched from the fire.
Away he sped with me in hot pursuit;
a chase that led straight to the White House grounds.

HYDE

What, did the fire then simply flicker out
without a reason? Hell aborting arson!
Why, even Nero fiddling never charmed
the snaking flames entangling ancient Rome
to cease their hissing; nor such luck snip through
the red- and white-hot black swastika's web
to keep the blazing Reichstag from collapse.
Are you sure there's not some mistake?

BOSKY

                                        None, sir.
Not a mistake: I saw it for myself.

LA BREA

Were nowhere flames by which you could have seen
the perpetrator's face reflected?

BOSKY

                                  No,
only his back, and from a distance too.
He sprinted like the wind and led me here.
No gate guard seemed on duty, no one asked
for proof of my identity, or his.

BOSKY (Continued)
With your permission, Mr. President,
I want to search the premises outside:
the culprit may be hiding quite near by.

HYDE
By all means, Agent Bosky, as you like.
Any incriminating skeletons
that you uncover I shall gladly dance with.

LA BREA
The President has nothing to conceal.

HYDE
Unless you were about to leave us, Doctor,
perhaps you would be good enough to help
the Agent in his search?

LA BREA
                              I wasn't leaving,
especially if the keepers at the gate
have somehow vanished. That we'll check outside.
At midnight I'll return: you may require
the services of your physician then.

(LA BREA and BOSKY move to the door.)

HYDE
Go, go.

(LA BREA and BOSKY go out. HYDE stares at a
clock on the wall. Through another door slips
WALDO with his revolver drawn.)

WALDO
This gun is loaded, Hyde. Put up your hands!
Don't move a muscle or I shoot to kill.

(HYDE raises his hands.)

HYDE
Waldo! I didn't expect you'd visit here.

WALDO
I had credentials: at the gate I flashed
this invitation that opens all doors.
Keep up your hands! From the asylum come
search parties and bloodhounds after me
that should be chasing you; they'd have by now
this evidence you torched, which sputtered out.

(WALDO displays a sealed box.)

This is the parcel I'm delivering, Hyde,
Special Delivery with your name on it.

HYDE
Crayoned by you then, when you picked it up.
I never saw that parcel in my life!

WALDO
Now dawns the day of judgement, Hyde. You made
a worthless paper of my mother's nest egg.
Nobody's safe while you still prowl the night.
I hated Mother, and I faint at blood,

(WALDO waves the gun.)

but with this loaded gun I have a stake
to stab your heart with! Vampire, dare become
a bat, I'll drill you with a silver bullet!

HYDE
But, Waldo, we've gone off the silver standard!

WALDO
Only because your program mounted up
tremendous debts by promising the moon
to men you hired to dig for gold and silver.

WALDO (Continued)
That wasn't panning out, so you began
your counterfeiting, as this package shows.
I'm making a citizen's arrest of you.
Whatever you say can be taken down
as evidence and used against you, Hyde.

HYDE
Alas, there isn't evidence against me.
The parcel's empty, Waldo. It contains
no proof admissible in any court,
only the spurious evidence I planted
to let me call my soul my own again,
because my villainy abhors a vacuum.
You see, I had to smother the recovery
with this red herring. I admit as much,
Now you must help in salvaging the plot.
Return the parcel, Waldo, where you found it.
Relight the fire, make it the fatal spark
for sending the economy to blazes.
Think of the chaos you could reignite!
You want that, Waldo; I can see you do.
Look in my eyes directly, and deny it.

WALDO
You'd hypnotize me then. I know that stare!

HYDE
That's only my charisma.

(HYDE advances, as WALDO backs up.)

WALDO
Keep away!

HYDE
Throw in your lot with me, or go to jail.

WALDO

I don't feel well; I'm getting very dizzy.
Stop weaving and stand still!
Isn't there any justice in the world?

HYDE

Nor in the next one either. To attempt
assassination for the sake of justice
avails you only outcomes in reverse.
Justice doesn't exist. How many times
has it been violated in our eyes
that we can only seek it in a dream
of art or fable! It's you who's weaving, Waldo!
To murder me would be absurd for justice,
and you should know it. Put the gun away.
To hit so small a target as my heart
would take a sharper marksmanship than yours.
And even if you managed wounding me,
the gore would drown you, spraying drops about
high as your eyeballs, hemorrhaging my words
on flowing blood as pythons with saliva
saturate prey for easy swallowing.
Forward I'd stumble wording on at you,
enveloping you in a lathering flow,
because, of course, I'm nothing if not wordy—

WALDO

Shut up! I'm getting dizzy from your talk!
Faint. Where am I? . . .

(A bell tolls.)

HYDE

Why hesitate? I'll shut my eyes and wait
to hear the trigger click its welcome bell,
as any wealthy man might ring his butler.

(WALDO sinks to the carpet. With eyes shut, HYDE
stands through the tolling of the bell.)

HYDE (Continued)
I hear death's dreaded knell, but is this all?
Can life be over? I open my eyes

(HYDE opens his eyes.)

expecting hell—But no: it's heaven still!

(HE stretches luxuriantly on the floor. In rush
BOSKY, FRANCES, LA BREA and LUCY.)

FRANCES
Oh, Mr. President, what is all this?
Have you been wounded?

HYDE
                    Only resting now.
Waldo just fainted too, as you can see.

BOSKY
Yes, he escaped the sanitarium,
and on the loose he likely tried to burn
the Herring warehouse down, and maybe even
has a connection with the forgeries.

(BOSKY notices the parcel.)

Look at this package maybe we should mark
Exhibit A, as evidence of that!

(BOSKY handcuffs WALDO and picks up the box.)

HYDE
No, no! That fool forged nothing, not a thing.
The parcel's empty.

LUCY
                    John, are you all right?

HYDE
Is it you, Lucy? But no sign of Helen.

BOSKY
Waldo's reviving finally.

WALDO
                    Where am I?

(BOSKY hoists WALDO up.)

BOSKY
Up on your feet, man! You're in custody!
And we'll get answers if we have to comb
the mansion grounds to get the truth on you
for counterfeiting, if it takes till winter.
Where you'll go, Waldo, people have the time
for bathing in the sun, but not the sun.
Doctor, I have my patient, you have yours.
Excuse us, ladies: me and Mr. Waldo
have business elsewhere.

LA BREA
                    Meanwhile you may leave
President Hyde in my hands, and be assured
he'll have the best of treatment.

BOSKY
                    Waldo, move!

WALDO
The government did it. I want a lawyer.

(BOSKY and WALDO go out.)

LUCY
Doctor, can't we do anything at all?

LA BREA
Unfortunately, madam, I believe
this patient to get better must grow worse.

LUCY
But I'm not budging, John. We'll see this through
together, past or not, as man and wife.
Forget divorce; we'll get you reëlected!
In the long run, we must be reconciled,
because toward you my heart has never changed.

HYDE
As weak as mine then; now no strength to change.
Anyway, in the long run we're all dead,
My plan is foiled, and everything is over.
There's nothing left to do if I recover.
Or, Frances, you will have to do it for me.

FRANCES
Yes, this is Frances, sir, telling you
of the good news about the civil trial
of Mrs. Scopes, whom in my court I rule
her teaching deficit expenditures
to local students legally sustained.
Verdict of the court acquits the lady.
The statute is unconstitutional.
Millions of dollars in appropriations
that you desired now Congress may approve
for building spacecraft that can reach the moon
and other planets. It's poetic justice.
Because the great depression came to men
as panic from the aether, to the aether
men now return. Congratulations, sir.

HYDE
Why is this happening? Oh, no more good news!
I'm dying of good news! . . .

(HYDE dies.)

LUCY

Oh!
Is that a death then? Is he really dead?

LA BREA

He played the jester to the very end,
and died at least acknowledging his triumph.

LUCY

But in that very moment to expire!

LA BREA

Believe me, Mrs. Hyde, that's the best way.
I've witnessed worse. Your Honor, will you see
the widow to her capsules and her rest?

FRANCES

Good night then, Doctor. Come on, Lucy: sleep.

LA BREA

Good night, good night. Leave the deceased to me.
On the horizon waits a new break of day.
After a long night spent, I must get home.
A doctor treats his patients in his office,
but Death makes house calls. Get to bed. Good night!

(LA BREA ushers them out, but blows a kiss to the audience.)

END OF THE PLAY

Biography of Ronald Garbin

The author started composing brief skits in graduate school, while studying physics at Wayne State University. He wrote a Masters essay on *Poincare's Relativistic Physics,* and a Ph.D thesis on *Transport Coefficients of a Diatomic Gas.* His first full-length stage comedy *The Wooden Horse* won a contest prize from the Greater Detroit Motion Picture Council. His second, *Great Tweed*, got accepted for publication by *First Stage.*

He taught for two years at the University of Windsor, then resigned to spend winter of 1969-70 in London, UK frequenting the Poetry Society at Earl's Court. Then the author added three more years at England's Players/Playwrights Society as its Program Secretary, scheduling and casting members' plays for staged readings, including his own, such as *A Perfect Stranger.* This comedy has a human-looking time bomb robot that claims itself no machine, but a hot-blooded poet in pursuit of its inventor's lady-love. An early, prose version of *John Hyde* got drafted also and staged.

Back in the U.S., the Treasury Department's Applied Math Lab employed Dr. Garbin in computer work, wholly new to him. Yet new plays also emerged. *Old Robert Broome,* starts with dénouement of a solved case backfiring on the know-it-all detective, plunging him into more puzzle, border smuggling, a lost parchment and/or its muse, and a search for perpetual youth. Then followed *Loafer Bees* about employees in a modern rural office, ranked semifinalist by Trustus Theatre in South Carolina.

Next came the Department of Agriculture (USDA), where the Office of Information Resources Management employed him, first as a Case Officer reviewing agency proposals, ultimately as Review Program Manager. This experience likewise newly exposed the citified author to basic issues often wonderfully conflicted and theatrical.

So the author's more recent scripts focus on conflicts of ecology and population. *In Future Perfect* a perhaps sun-stroked scientist claims abduction from the desert by time travelers escaping an environmentally wrecked future earth. *Safe Houses*, tells of a group in conflict over its fostered influx of foreigners in face of their country's rising border wall. *Vikki's Ladder* dramatizes a so-called War on Coincidence launched when an aspiring playwright's script foretells with uncanny accuracy a terrorist attack that stirs official suspicions of the playwright.

Several summers ago the Pend Oreille Players in Newport, Washington State, staged his short play *The Reservation*. The plot resulted from a dream (or comic nightmare) the author had, of a condemned man escorted to a posh restaurant on the night of his last meal.

The author suspects easy solutions, and hopes dramatic conflict still exists, and that *John Hyde* proves it.

www.ingramcontent.com/pod-product-compliance
Lightning Source LLC
Chambersburg PA
CBHW021154090426
42740CB00008B/1082